Bron Johnson

THE

WOOD PELLET SMOKER & GRILL

COOKBOOK SERIES

SERIAL GRILLER

The total wood pellet smoker cookbook with juicy recipes to turn every beginner into the complete pitmaster

- THE -

EST. **OLD** 1999
TEXAS
PITMASTER

TRAVIS COUNTY

Recipes by Bron Johnson

Photography: Humbert Castillo

Graphic design: Tori Vergara

Editorial coordination: Joe Garcia and Humbert Castillo

First edition March 2021

CONTENTS

ABOUT BRON JOHNSON

Author of "The Wood Pellet Grill Cookbook", Bron has spent most of his life smelling of wood-fired smoke. Bron wasn't always a professional pitmaster. He spent years as a commercial banker, and it was his bank that would eventually lead him to BBQ. The bank held a BBQ competition every year, and as an adamant griller, Bron felt he'd be able to hold his own. Once the competition started, he was in awe of the whole culture.

Teams smoking meat, drinking beer, and telling stories. Growing up in the South, he knew BBQ, but the culture around the competition added a whole new level of inspiration.

Before retiring in 1999, he served his Country in the Military. Bronson has two sons and two grandchildren. He lives in Austin, Texas, with his wife of 59 years. When not in the backyard smoking, roasting & grilling meats, he can be found tending his vegetable garden, fishing, or golfing. Peter and his wife enjoy traveling the Country in their RV - but he never leaves home without his tailgate portable wood pellet smoker-grill.

INTRODUCTION

A wood pellet grill uses proprietary wood pellets as fuel. This is different from a wood grill, and especially a charcoal grill.

Joe Traeger is the inventor of the wood pellet grill. He came up with the idea after he noticed his gas grill was in flames as he was preparing to cook for his family. That was in 1988. Today, pellet grills give consumers the flavor of wood smoke with the conve- nience of a gas grill.

Benefits of a Pellet Grill

We already know that pellet grills can be used to smoke, grill, bake and even braise food, and with all those capabilities it's no surprise that they act more like an outdoor oven than a traditional grill. The options for what to cook on a pellet grill are nearly endless because unlike other grills or smokers, a pellet grill allows you to cook something low and slow — or hotter and faster. You can also set a specific temperature which makes for consistent, efficient cooking every time. With no direct heat cooking and no open flame, you don't even have to worry about flare- ups!

Wood Pellet Grill vs. Gas Grill

The biggest difference between a pellet grill and a gas grill: the flavor! Pellet grills are powered by hardwood pellets and thus impart a naturally sweet, spicy, smoky flavor to everything you cook; a flavor that is unmatched by cooking on gas or charcoal grills. The team at Traeger says: *"The smoke acts as a wholly separate seasoning, adding a deeper and more robust flavor to whatever you decide to cook"*.

The flavor of cooking with wood pellets doesn't even compare to the flavor of cooking on a gas grill. Sure, you can argue that cooking over an open flame like you would on a gas grill gives off flavor, but what if you could get that meaty, smoky flavor without the inevitable ashy, burnt and blackened taste? That's where your pellet grill comes in. Heat is generated through combustion, by igniting wood pellets and circulating heat through a fan system. Much like a convection oven, this allows us to set and maintain a specific temperature
without worrying about the unpredictability of open fire flare-ups.

Wood Pellet Grill vs. Charcoal Grill

Although charcoal grills are certainly known for smoky flavor, there's one major difference that sets pellet grills apart from their charcoal counterpart: temperature regulation. Whatever temperature you decide to set your pellet grill to, you can be certain that it will maintain it. One of the biggest downfalls of a charcoal grill is that although it can achieve high temperatures, it's difficult to maintain high temperatures. We've all been there; you've heated your coals to the perfect temperature and before you know it, they're cooling off again! Pellet grills allow you to set a specific cooking temperature (some even support the use of an internal therm- ometer that pairs with your Bluetooth), so you can check on the doneness of your meat from the comfort of your couch. This system makes for a much more predictable, manageable and convenient grilling experience.

Overall, pellet grills are an exciting advancement in barbecuing. Most commonly known as "smokers," these grills are powered by hardwood pellets and act more like an outdoor oven than a standard gas or charcoal grill.
Wood pellet grills are one of the hottest trends in grilling right now. If you just got one or are about to, you've no doubt wondered how to use a wood pellet grill.

Wood pellet grills use real wood, all-natural wood pellets as fuel but also req uire an electrical outlet for power. Unlike propane, natural gas, or charcoal grills, burning pellets is not harmful to the environment. They come in a variety of flavors and are FDA approved.

Let's get started!

MEAT CUTS

PORK

Pork might not be my favorite meat, but it just might be my best. I have spent hours in front of my grill, prepping ribs and pork shoulders. As a frequent host of large parties, including a yearly rematch of Bad Santa with my hooligan high school friends, I had to start somewhere — and pork was a great place to start.

Pork has a salty flavor that cannot be mistaken. Though it can get in the way at times, the fat content in pork allows it to be both juicy and tender.

Pork goes exceptionally well with sweet flavors, and I refer to that a lot. Pick up some local honey; it supports the beekeepers, farmers, and markets in the area. Plus, local honey tastes better. Brown sugar is delicious with pork, too. And whenever I visit a buddy in Toronto, I always pick up some Canadian maple syrup in the duty-free shop on the way home to have on hand for pork recipes.

1. Head
2. Clear Plate
3. Back Fat
4. Boston Butt/Shoulder
5. Loin/Tenderloin
6. Ham
7. Cheek
8. Picnic Shoulder
9. Ribs
10. Bacon/Belly
11. Hock

RIBS

Ribs, particularly baby back ribs, are my best dish. If there's one thing I do as well as James LeBron throws a basketball, it's smoking ribs. I will speak in general terms when dealing with pork ribs, spare ribs, and baby backs. You want to select a cut with a good amount of fat in both cases, but it should be consistent throughout. Too much fat, especially if it is only in certain places, can make for an unappetizingly fatty bite.

We will prep our ribs the way you see them at a competition, not at the local chain barbecue restaurant. These will have just the slightest pull. To them just before the meat slips and falls off the bone. If you want the meat slipping and sliding off the bone, cook them a little longer.

TIPS & TECHNIQUES

Remove the membrane. That weird membrane on the back of ribs (sometimes called silver skin) can make them harder to pull off the bone and less tender. To get pit master-level results each time, remove the membrane.

Use mustard as a binder. Mustard works excellent as a binder for your rub on fatty meats such as ribs. Rub plain yellow mustard or another smooth mustard over your ribs before or after your rub. This will keep your rub on your meat and not all over your drip pan. Use whatever liquid you like best (including beer or wine, but not liquor) for your spritz or your wrap. When watching a competition cook prep ribs with Mountain Dew, I asked why. "It's what my brother and I like and what we had, so we just started using it," he told me. I use Pepsi; my dad and brother use apple juice. Use what you like, or see what other pitmasters are using and try that for a change. It's a great place to experiment.

Sauce it—just don't overdo it. Again, saucing is a natural preference. At parties, I always have a plate of ribs with just a dry rub. Over the years, my ribs have gone from dry to heavily sauced, and now I just use a light sweet coating. As you will see in the recipes, we also have other ways to achieve sweetness.

Country-style ribs are ribs. Cook boneless country-style ribs the same way you would other ribs. The smoked flavor is excellent, and they are incredibly tender when done.

PORK SHOULDER

Pulled pork is something pit masters love. Not just because it's easy and good, but because it typically means leftovers for days. Sliders, nachos, and sandwiches are all day-two and day-three renditions of the pulled-pork-leftover week. A good-size pork shoulder could feed an army—or at least an army of kids just back from baseball, gymnastics, or soccer. When selecting your pork shoulder—also called pork

Butt or Boston butt—it doesn't matter if you choose one with or without a bone. However, do check the fat content. You want some fat, or your pork will dry out, but too much can be overly fatty, just like ribs. The fat cap should be less than 1 inch deep.

TIPS & TECHNIQUES

Inject your pork shoulder for extra moisture and flavor. Using tea, inject your shoulder. A good shoulder will have a nice flavorful bark, but injecting will give it flavor everywhere.

Smoke your pork longer for a good "bark." The bark isn't just on trees or what your dog does. The bark is that delicious crust on the outside of well-smoked meat. The bark develops when the meat and rub are combined with uninterrupted smoke for an extended time. A good pork shoulder will have a good, dark bark. To increase the amount of bark, smoke the pork longer, unwrapped.

Use your hands when pulling the meat— it's just easier. There are some new cool claws available that can be used for pulling pork. They keep your hands from getting hot and greasy. Fact is, though, with those, the pull never really feels right. I have a pair of gloves I wear under food service gloves. The gloves keep my hands from burning but let me pull the meat precisely as I like it.

TENDERLOINS

Pork tenderloins are among the simplest smoke pre- partitions on the grill, but they're always impressive. I smoke a couple of tenderloins for my family every couple of weeks, and they never get tired of them. The pellet grill or smoker does a fantastic job with tenderloins, ensuring a juicy result each time.

When selecting tenderloins, as with most pork, the key is fat content. I try to limit the fat content on my tenderloins. A pellet grill will work to keep them moist and will limit dried-out areas.

TIPS & TECHNIQUES

If you're lazy, just smoke them. The Smoke setting of the pellet grill works great to get your meat to

The temperature while always keeping it moist. Use a reverse sear. Searing is usually done first, before cooking the meat entirely. When we do it last, after fully smoking the meat, we call it a reverse sear.

If your grill has an open flame option, like a flame broiler, use that; otherwise, crank up your grill's temperature as high as it will go.

After smoking the tenderloins until their internal temperature reaches 135°F to 140°F, sear them off at a higher temperature until they reach 145°F, about 3 to 5 minutes per side. Pork tenderloins are a great candidate for marinating. Teriyaki-marinated pork tenderloin tastes fantastic, and the meat can take on the marinade flavor in as little as 30 minutes.

BEEF

When I think of smoking and barbecue, my mind immediately goes to beef: significant cuts of brisket and tri-tip, steaks over a flame. Fortunately, with today's grill technology, all of these are possible on a pellet grill. But the dream of so many pitmasters is that perfect Texas-style brisket. We have all spent hours researching how best to achieve it: Wrapped or unwrap- ped? Foil or butcher paper? How long should it take? We also want steaks that even the owner of the best steakhouse would pay for—the smoke and the butter and the fire, all infused with the smell of searing meat. That's what we aim for in our backyards.

This is why I think "beef" when I think of smoking and barbecue. Selecting beef is made more accessible by its grade. We'll go into this here, as well as some other tips to make you a master of low-and-slow meat cooking.

1.   Neck
2.   Chuck
3.   Rib
4.   Short Loin
5.   Sirloin
6.   Tenderloin
7.   Top Sirloin

8.   Rump Cap
9.   Round
10.   Brisket
11.   Shoulder Clod
12.   Short Plate
13.   Flank

BRISKET

In my experience, brisket tends to be the gold standard and the most difficult to cook on the pellet grill. Many look at the perfect brisket with reverence and hope for the day when they'll successfully achieve it. Discussions fill message boards on the bend test, the pull test, and the like. The problem with this line of thinking around brisket? Well, it's actually not that difficult to make! Brisket, just like anything else, can be perfected with practice and patience.

When selecting the perfect brisket—and I am referring- ring to a whole brisket, with both the point and flat cuts (usually separated at most butchers) intact— the key is not too fat. If you buy a brisket with a huge fat cap, you are just going to cut it off. Also, I suggest spending the extra money on the highest grade of brisket available to you. A cheap brisket can equal a tough brisket. Brisket is not a cheap cut anyway, so spend the money for the best cut.

TIPS & TECHNIQUES

Get rid of that fat cap. A large fat cap is just not appetizing if you leave it on when you smoke your brisket. Use a boning knife or whatever knife you have available and cut the fat cap down to about ¼ inch. Trimming the fat cap will decrease the fattiness of your brisket, but leaving it partially there will keep the meat moist.

Wrap, don't wrap. You choose. Both aluminum foil and butcher paper can be used for wrapping—again, it is all about preference. However, I will say about wrapping because it doesn't do it until after the stall, 165°F to 170°F. Wrapping too early cuts down on your bark development, and your brisket won't be as smoky.

If you don't wrap the meat, spritz it or use a water pan. Spritzing with liquid, like apple juice or plain water, will ensure your brisket stays moist. A water pan can be used in a pellet grill just like you would in any other type of grill, but be careful not to spill it. Simply fill a metal pan with water and place it inside the grill. Have a flat drain pan; the water pan will sit.

Let's Get Cooking!

MEAT RECIPES

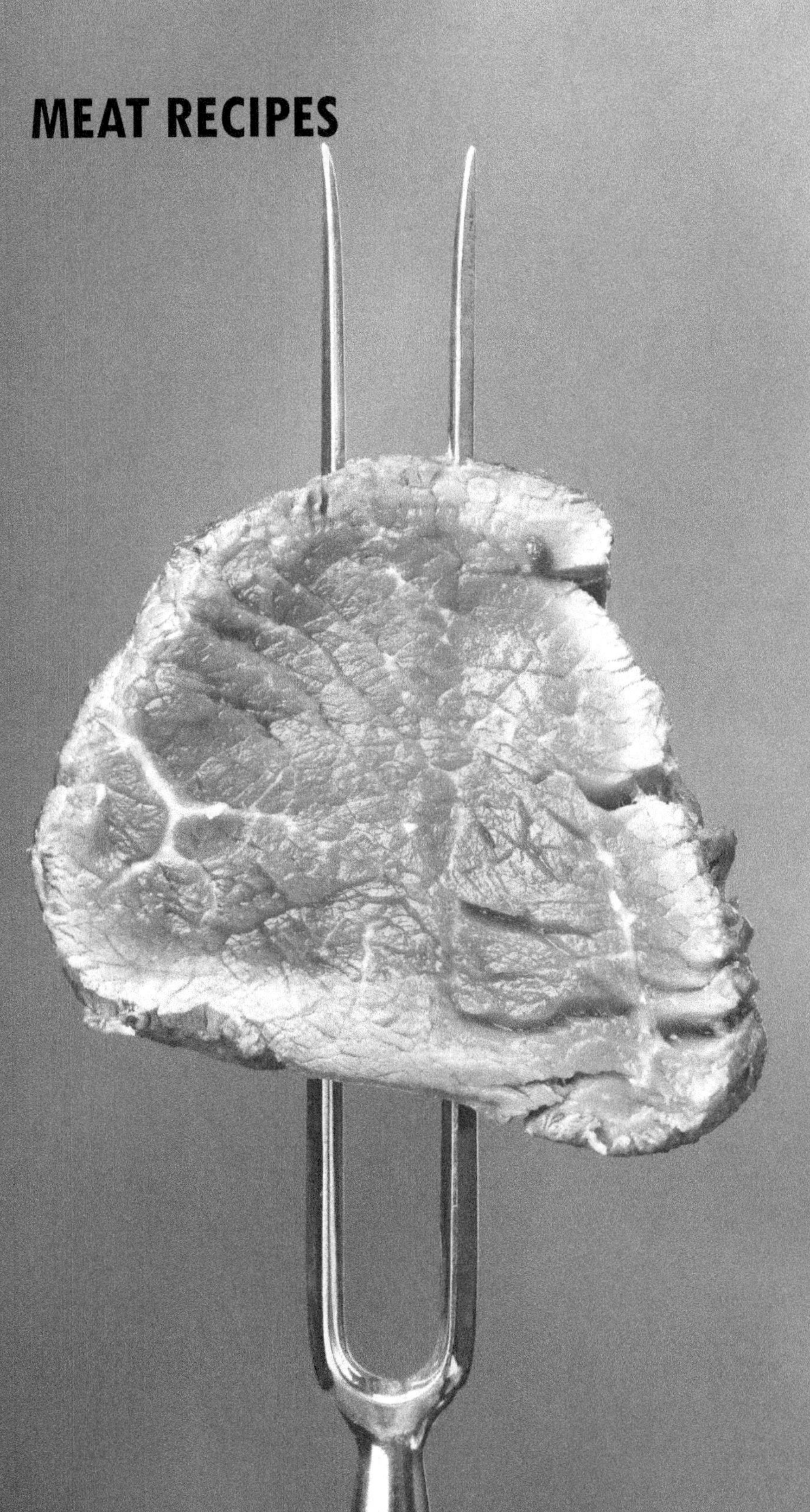

Smoked and Pulled Beef

Preparation Time: 10 minutes | Cooking Time: 6 hours | Servings: 6

- 4 lb. beef sirloin tip roast
- 1/2 cup BBQ rub
- 2 bottles of amber beer 1 bottle barbecues sauce

Turn your wood pellet grill on smoke setting then trim excess fat from the steak.

Coat the steak with BBQ rub and let it smoke on the grill for 1 hour. Continue cooking and flipping the steak for the next 3 hours. Transfer the steak to a braising vessel. Add the beers.

Braise the beef until tender then transfer to a platter reserving 2 cups of cooking liquid.

Use a pair of forks to shred the beef and return it to the pan. Add the reserved liquid and barbecue sauce. Stir well and keep warm before serving.

Enjoy.

Wood Pellet Smoked Brisket

Preparation Time: 20 minutes | Cooking Time: 9 hours | Servings: 10

- 2 tbsp garlic powder
- 2 tbsp onion powder
- 2 tbsp paprika
- 2 tbsp chili powder
- 1/3 cup salt
- 1/3 cup black pepper
- 12 lb whole packer brisket, trimmed
- 1-1/2 cup beef broth

Set your wood pellet temperature to 225°F. Let preheat for 15 minutes with the lid closed.

Meanwhile, mix garlic, onion, paprika, chili, salt, and pepper in a mixing bowl.

Season the brisket generously on all sides.

Place the meat on the grill with the fat side down and let it cool until the internal temperature reaches 160°F. Remove the meat from the grill and double wrap it with foil. Return it to the grill and cook until the internal temperature reaches 204°F.

Remove from the grill, unwrap the brisket, and let sit for 15 minutes. Slice and serve.

Traeger Beef Jerky

Preparation Time: 15 minutes | Cooking Time: 5 hours | Servings: 10

- 3 lb. sirloin steaks
- 2 cups soy sauce
- 1 cup pineapple juice
- 1/2 cup brown sugar
- 2 tbsp sriracha
- 2 tbsp hoisin
- 2 tbsp red pepper flake
- 2 tbsp rice wine vinegar
- 2 tbsp onion powder

Mix the marinade in a zip lock bag and add the beef. Mix until well coated and remove as much air as possible.

Place the bag in a fridge and let marinate overnight or for 6 hours. Remove the bag from the fridge an hour before cooking 3) Startup the Traeger and set it on the smoking settings or at 1900F.

Lay the meat on the grill leaving a half-inch space between the pieces. Let cool for 5 hours and turn after 2 hours. Remove from the grill and let cool. Serve or refrigerate

Smoked Beef Roast

Preparation Time: 10 minutes | Cooking Time: 6 hours | Servings: 6

- 1-3/4 lb. beef sirloin tip roast
- 1/2 cup BBQ rub
- 2 bottles of amber beer
- 1 bottle BBQ sauce

Turn the wood pellet grill onto the smoke setting.

Transfer the beef to a pan and add the beer. The beef should be 1/2 way covered.

Braise the beef until fork tender. It will take 3 hours on the stovetop and 60 minutes on the instant pot.

Remove the beef from the ban and reserve 1 cup of the cooking liquid. Use 2 forks to shred the beef into small pieces then return to the pan with the reserved braising liquid.

Add BBQ sauce and stir well then keep warm until serving. You can also reheat if it gets cold.

Reverse Seared Flank Steak

Preparation Time: 10 minutes | Cooking Time: 20 minutes | Servings:2

- 3 lb. flank steaks
- 1 tbsp salt
- 1/2 tbsp onion powder 1/4 tbsp garlic powder
- 1/2 black pepper, coarsely ground

Preheat the wood pellet grill to 225F.

All the ingredients in a bowl and mix well. Add the steaks and rub them generously with the rub mixture. Place the steak on the grill and close the lid. Let cook until its internal temperature is 100F under your desired temperature. 115F for rare, 125F for the medium rear, and 135F for medium.

Wrap the steak with foil and raise the grill temperature to high. Place back the steak and grill for 3 minutes on each side. Pat with butter and serve when hot.

Beef Tenderloin

Preparation Time: 10 minutes | Cooking Time: 45 minutes | Servings:6

- 4 lb. beef tenderloin
- 3 tbsp steak rub 1 tbsp kosher salt

Preheat the wood pellet grill to high heat. Meanwhile, trim excess fat from the beef and cut it into 3 pieces. Coat the steak with rub and kosher salt. Place it on the grill.
Close the lid and cook for 10 minutes. Open the lid, flip the beef and cook for 10 more minutes. Reduce the temperature of the grill to 225F and smoke the beef until the internal temperature reaches 130F.

Remove the beef from the grill and let rest for 15 minutes before slicing and serving.

New York Strip

Preparation Time: 5 minutes | Cooking Time: 15 minutes | Servings: 6

- 3 New York strips
- Salt and pepper

If the steak is in the fridge, remove it 30 minutes before cooking. Preheat the wood pellet grill to 450F.

Meanwhile, season the steak generously with salt and pepper. Place it on the grill and let it cook for 5 minutes per side or until the internal temperature reaches 120F.

Remove the steak from the grill and let it rest for 10 minutes.

Traeger Stuffed Peppers

Preparation Time: 20 minutes | Cooking Time: 5 minutes | Servings: 6

- 3 bell peppers, sliced in halves
- 1 lb. ground beef, lean
- 1 onion, chopped
- 1/2 tbsp red pepper flakes
- 1/2 tbsp salt
- 1/4 tbsp pepper
- 1/2 tbsp garlic powder
- 1/2 tbsp onion powder
- 1/2 cup white rice
- 15 oz stewed tomatoes
- 8 oz tomato sauce
- 6 cups cabbage, shredded
- 1-1/2 cup water 2 cups cheddar cheese

Arrange the pepper halves on a baking tray and set aside.

Preheat your grill to 325F.

Brown the meat in a large skillet. Add onions, pepper flakes, salt, pepper garlic, and onion and cook until the meat is well cooked.

Add rice, stewed tomatoes, tomato sauce, cabbage, and water.

Cover and simmer until the rice is well cooked, the cabbage is tender and there is no water in the rice.

Place the cooked beef mixture in the pepper halves and top with cheese.

Place in the grill and cook for 30 minutes.

Serve immediately and enjoy it.

Prime Rib Roast

Preparation Time: 10 minutes | Cooking Time: 2 hours | Servings: 8

- 5 lb. rib roast, boneless
- 4 tbsp salt
- 1 tbsp black pepper
- 1-1/2 tbsp onion powder
- 1 tbsp granulated garlic
- 1 tbsp rosemary
- 1 cup chopped onion
- 1/2 cup carrots, chopped
- 1/2 cup celery, chopped
- 2 cups beef broth

Remove the beef from the fridge 1 hour before cooking.

Preheat the wood pellet grill to 250F.

In a small mixing bowl, mix salt, pepper, onion, garlic, and rosemary to create your rub.

Generously coat the roast with the rub and set it aside.

Combine chopped onions, carrots, and celery in a cake pan then place the bee on top.

Place the cake pan in the middle of the Traeger and cook for 1 hour.

Pour the beef broth at the bottom of the cake pan and cook until the internal temperature reaches 120F.

Remove the cake pan from the Traeger and let rest for 20 minutes before slicing the meat.

Pour the cooking juice through a strainer, then skim off any fat at the top.

Serve the roast with the cooking juices.

Fine Indian Smoked T-Bone

Preparation Time20 minutes | Cooking Time:45 minutes | Servings: 12

- 1-pound beef tenderloin, cut into 1-inch cubes
- 2 pounds strip steak, cut into 1-inch cubes
- 1 large onion, cut into 1-inch cubes
- 1 bell pepper, cut into 1-inch cubes
- 1 zucchini, cut into 1-inch cubes
- 10 ounces cherry tomatoes
- ¼ cup olive oil ½ cup steak seasoning

Take a large bowl and add tenderloin, strip steak, onion, zucchini, bell pepper, tomatoes and mix well with olive oil

Season with steak seasoning and stir until the meat has been coated well

Cover the meat and allow it to refrigerate for 4-8 hours

Preheat your smoker to 225 degrees Fahrenheit using your desired wood

Make the kebabs by skewering meat and veggies alternatively Make sure, to begin with, meat and end with meat Transfer the skewers to your smoker rack and smoke for 45 minutes

Remove once the internal temperature reaches 135 degrees Fahrenheit (for a RARE finish) Serve and enjoy!

The South Barbacoa

Preparation Time: 15 minutes | Cooking Time: 3 hours | Servings: 10

- 1 and ½ teaspoon pepper
- 1 tablespoon dried oregano
- 1 and ½ teaspoon cayenne pepper
- 1 and ½ teaspoon chili powder
- 1 and ½ teaspoon garlic powder
- 1 teaspoon ground cumin
- 1 teaspoon salt
- 3 pounds boneless beef chuck roast

Add dampened hickory wood to your smoker and preheat to 200 degrees Fahrenheit
Take a small bowl and add oregano, cayenne pepper, black pepper, garlic powder, chili powder, cumin, salt, and seasoned salt
Mix well
Dip the chuck roast into your mixing bowl and rub the spice mix all over
Transfer the meat to your smoker and smoker for 1 and a ½ hours
Make sure to turn the meat after every 30 minutes, if you see less smoke formation, add more Pellets after every 30 minutes as well
Once the meat shows a dark red color with darkened edges, transfer the meat to a roasting pan and seal it tightly with an aluminum foil
Preheat your oven to 325 degrees Fahrenheit
Transfer the meat to your oven and bake for 1 and a ½ hours more
Shred the meat using two forks and serve!

Smoked Prime Rib

Preparation Time: 25 minutes | Cooking Time: 4 hours | Servings: 12

- 1 whole (8 pounds) prime rib roast
- 2 onions, thickly sliced
- Smoked teriyaki marinade
- Salt as needed
- Fresh ground pepper as needed

Take a large container and add meat and marinade

Combine onion slices and pour cover well

Marinade for 2 hours

Turn the meat over then cover it, refrigerate for 2 hours more Preheat your smoker to 225 degrees Fahrenheit using oak wood Remove the roast and onions from the container and discard the marinade

Skewer the onion slices making "onion lollipops" Season the rib with pepper and salt, and transfer the meat and skewered onion to your smoker rack Smoke for 4-6 hours

Remove the meat when the internal temperature reaches 135 degrees Fahrenheit Allow it to rest for 15 minutes and serve!

Braised BBQ Ribs

Prep time: 5 minutes | Cook time: 5 hours 10 minutes | Serves 4

- 2 rack St. Louis-style ribs, patted dry and membrane removed
- ¼ cup Traeger Big Game Rub
- 1 cup apple juice
- Traeger BBQ Sauce, as needed

1. Brush the ribs all over with the Traeger Big Game Rub. Let marinate for 20 minutes and up to 4 hours if refrigerated.
2. When ready to cook, set wood pellet grill temperature to 225°F (107°C) and preheat, lid closed for 15 minutes.
3. Arrange the ribs, bone-side down, on the grill and cook for 5 hours.
4. After 1 hour, put the apple juice in a spray bottle and spritz the ribs. Spritz every 45 minutes thereafter.
5. After 4½ hours, check the internal temperature of ribs. The ribs are done when the internal temperature reaches 200°F (93°C). If not, check back in another 30 minutes.
6. When done, brush the ribs all over with the Traeger BBQ Sauce. Cook for 10 more minutes to set the sauce.
7. Remove the ribs from the grill and let rest for 10 minutes. Slice the ribs in between the bones and serve warm.

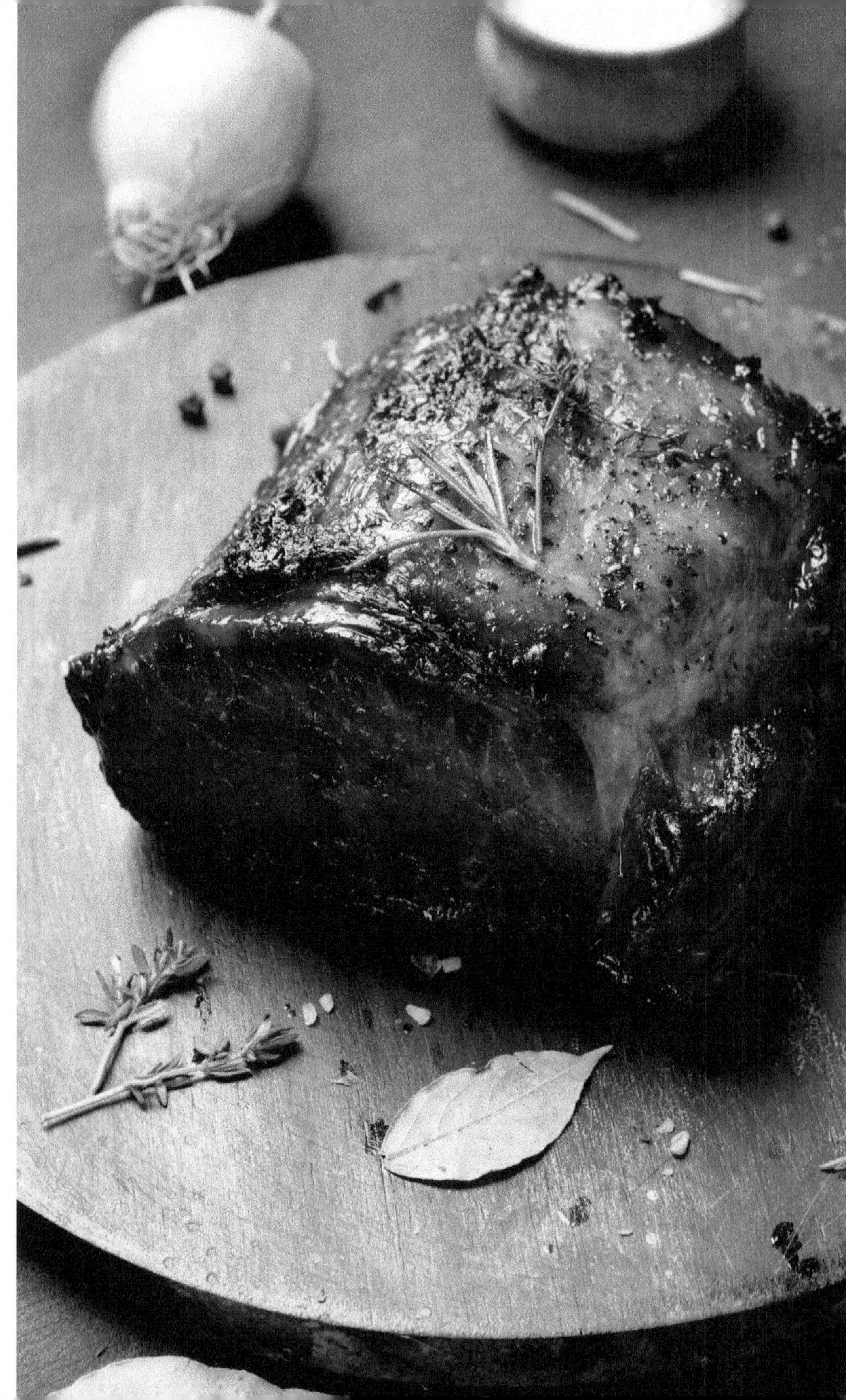

Apricot BBQ Smoked Pork Tenderloin

Prep time: 5 minutes | Cook time: 48 minutes | Serves 4

- 2 pounds (907 g) pork tenderloin, trimmed
- 3 ounces (85 g) Traeger Big Game Rub
- 1 cup Traeger Apricot BBQ Sauce

1. Brush the pork tenderloin all over with the Traeger Big Game Rub and let marinate for 30 minutes.
2. When ready to cook, set wood pellet grill temperature to 180°F (82°C) and preheat, lid closed for 15 minutes.
3. Arrange the pork tenderloin on the grill grate and smoke for 45 minutes.
4. Remove the pork from the grill. Set Traeger temperature to High and preheat, lid closed for 15 minutes.
5. Place the pork back to the grill grate and grill each side of the pork tenderloin for 90 seconds, or until an instant-read thermometer inserted in the thickest part of the meat registers 145°F (63°C).
6. Brush the pork with the Traeger Apricot BBQ Sauce. Transfer to a plate and let cool for 20 minutes before serving.

Brown Sugar Baked Pork Belly

Prep time: 5 minutes | Cook time: 2o to 30 minutes | Serves 2

- ½ cup brown sugar
- 1 tablespoon ground fennel
- 2 teaspoons kosher salt
- 1 teaspoon ground black pepper
- 1 pound (454 g) pork belly, diced

1. Fold a piece of aluminum foil in half and crimp the edges so there is a rim. Using a fork, poke holes in the bottom of the foil.
2. When ready to cook, set Traeger temperature to 350°F (177°C) and preheat, lid closed for 15 minutes.
3. In a large bowl, stir together all the ingredients, except for the pork belly.
4. Add the diced pork belly to the bowl and toss until well coated. Transfer the pork pieces to the foil.
5. Place the foil on the grill and bake for 20 to 30 minutes, or until the pork belly is crispy, glazed and bubbly.
6. Let rest for 5 minutes before serving.

Delicious BBQ Lamb

Prep time: 1 hour | Cook time: 1 to 2 hours | Serves 4

- 2 racks of lamb, trimmed, frenched, and tied into a crown
- 1¼ cups extra-virgin olive oil, divided 2 tablespoons chopped fresh basil
- 2 tablespoons chopped fresh rosemary
- 2 tablespoons ground sage
- 2 tablespoons ground thyme
- 8 garlic cloves, minced
- 2 teaspoons salt
- 2 teaspoons freshly ground black pepper

1. Set the lamb out on the counter to take the chill off, about an hour.
2. In a small bowl, combine 1 cup of olive oil, the basil, rosemary, sage, thyme, garlic, salt, and pepper.
3. Baste the entire crown with the herbed olive oil and wrap the exposed frenched bones in aluminum foil.
4. Supply your smoker with wood pellets and follow the manufacturer's specific start-up procedure. Preheat, with the lid closed, to 275°F (135°C).
5. Put the lamb directly on the grill, close the lid, and smoke for 1 hour 30 minute to 2 hours, or until a meat thermometer inserted in the thickest part reads 140°F (60°C).
6. Remove the lamb from the heat, tent with foil, and let rest for about 15 minutes before serving. The temperature will rise about 5°F (-15°C) during the rest period, for a finished temperature of 145°F (63°C).

Smoked Venison Steaks

Prep time: 20 minutes | Cook time: 1 hour 20 minute | Serves 4

- 4 (8-ounce / 227-g) venison steaks
- 2 tablespoons extra-virgin olive oil
- 4 garlic cloves, minced
- 1 tablespoon ground sage
- 2 teaspoons sea salt
- 2 teaspoons freshly ground black pepper

1. Supply your smoker with wood pellets and follow the manufacturer's specific start-up procedure. Preheat, with the lid closed, to 225°F (107°C).
2. Rub the venison steaks well with the olive oil and season with the garlic, sage, salt, and pepper.
3. Arrange the venison steaks directly on the grill grate, close the lid, and smoke for 1 hour and 20 minute, or until a meat thermometer inserted in the center reads 130°F (54°C) to 140°F (60°C), depending on desired doneness. If you want a better sear, remove the steaks from the grill at an internal temperature of 125°F (52°C), crank up the heat to 450°F (232°C), or the "High" setting, and cook the steaks on each side for an additional 2 to 3 minutes.

Smoked Brats with Buds

Prep time: 10 minutes | Cook time: 1 to 2 hours | Serves 12 to 15

- 4 (12-ounce / 340-g) cans of beer
- 2 onions, sliced into rings
- 2 green bell peppers, sliced into rings
- 2 tablespoons unsalted butter, plus more for the rolls
- 2 tablespoons red pepper flakes
- 10 brats, uncooked
- 10 hoagie rolls, split
- Mustard, for serving

1. On your kitchen stove top, in a large saucepan over high heat, bring the beer, onions, peppers, butter, and red pepper flakes to a boil.
2. Supply your smoker with wood pellets and follow the manufacturer's specific start-up procedure. Preheat, with the lid closed, to 225°F (107°C).
3. Place a disposable pan on one side of grill, and pour the warmed beer mixture into it, creating a "brat tub" (see Tip below).
4. Place the brats on the other side of the grill, directly on the grate, and close the lid and smoke for 1 hour, turning 2 or 3 times.
5. Add the brats to the pan with the onions and peppers, cover tightly with aluminum foil, and continue smoking with the lid closed for 30 minute to 1 hour, or until a meat thermometer inserted in the brats reads 160°F (71°C).
6. Butter the cut sides of the hoagie rolls and toast cut-side down on the grill.
7. Using a slotted spoon, remove the brats, onions, and peppers from the cooking liquid and discard the liquid.
8. Serve the brats on the toasted buns, topped with the onions and peppers and mustard

Smoked Baby Back Ribs

Preparation Time: 10 minutes

Cooking Time 2 hours

Servings: 6

Ingredients:

- 3 racks baby back ribs Salt and pepper to taste

Directions:

Clean the ribs by removing the extra membrane that covers it. Pat dry the ribs with a clean paper towel. Season the baby back ribs with salt and pepper to taste. Allow resting in the fridge for at least 4 hours before cooking.

Once ready to cook, fire the wood pellet grill to 225F. Use hickory wood pellets when cooking the ribs. Close the lid and preheat for 15 minutes.

Place the ribs on the grill grate and cook for two hours. Carefully flip the ribs halfway through the cooking time for even cooking.

Smoked Pork Tenderloin

Preparation Time: 10 minutes

Cooking Time: 3 hours

Servings: 6 Ingredients: ½ cup apple juice

- 3 tablespoons honey
- 3 tablespoons Traeger Pork and Poultry Rub
- ¼ cup brown sugar
- 2 tablespoons thyme leaves
- ½ tablespoons black pepper
- 2 pork tenderloin roasts, skin removed

Directions:

In a bowl, mix the apple juice, honey, pork and poultry rub, brown sugar, thyme, and black pepper. Whisk to mix everything.

Add the pork loins into the marinade and allow it to soak for 3 hours in the fridge.

Once ready to cook, fire the wood pellet grill to 225F. Use hickory wood pellets when cooking the ribs. Close the lid and preheat for 15 minutes.

Place the marinated pork loin on the grill grate and cook until the temperature registers to 145F. Cook for 2 to 3 hours on low heat.

Meanwhile, place the marinade in a saucepan. Place the saucepan in the grill and allow it to simmer until the sauce has reduced.

Before taking the meat out, baste the pork with the reduced marinade.

Allow resting for 10 minutes before slicing.

Competition Style BBQ Pork Ribs

Preparation Time: 10 minutes

Cooking Time: 2 hours

Servings: 6

Ingredients:

- 2 racks of St. Louis-style ribs
- 1 cup Traeger Pork and Poultry Rub
- 1/8 cup brown sugar
- 4 tablespoons butter
- 4 tablespoons agave
- 1 bottle Traeger Sweet and Heat BBQ Sauce

Directions:

Place the ribs on the working surface and remove the thin film of connective tissues covering it. In a smaller bowl, combine the Traeger Pork and Poultry Rub, brown sugar, butter, and agave. Mix until well combined.

Massage the rub onto the ribs and allow them to rest in the fridge for at least 2 hours.

When ready to cook, fire the wood pellet grill to 220F. Use desired wood pellets when cooking the ribs. Close the lid and preheat for 15 minutes.

Place the ribs on the grill grate and close the lid. Smoke for 1 hour and 30 minutes. Make sure to flip the ribs halfway through the cooking time.

Ten minutes before the cooking time ends, brush the ribs with BBQ sauce.

Remove from the grill and allow to rest before slicing.

Easy Ribs

Preparation Time: 10 minutes

Cooking Time: 2 hours

Servings: 6

Ingredients:

- 2 racks St. Louis-style ribs
- ¼ cup Traeger Big Game Rub
- 1 cup apple juice
- A bottle of Traeger BBQ Sauce

Directions:

Place the ribs on a working surface and remove the film of connective tissues covering it.

In another bowl, mix the Game Rub and apple juice until well-combined.

Massage the rub onto the ribs and allow them to rest in the fridge for at least 2 hours.

When ready to cook, fire the wood pellet grill to 220F. Use apple wood pellets when cooking the ribs. Close the lid and preheat for 15 minutes.

Place the ribs on the grill grate and close the lid. Smoke for 1 hour and 30 minutes. Make sure to flip the ribs halfway through the cooking time.

Ten minutes before the cooking time ends, brush the ribs with BBQ sauce.

Remove from the grill and allow to rest before slicing.

Citrus-Brined Pork Roast

Preparation Time: 10 minutes

Cooking Time: 45 minutes

Servings: 6

Ingredients:

- ½ cup of salt
- ¼ cup brown sugar
- 3 cloves of garlic, minced
- 2 dried bay leaves
- 6 peppercorns
- 1 lemon, juiced
- ½ teaspoon dried fennel seeds
- ½ teaspoon red pepper flakes
- ½ cup of apple juice
- ½ cup of orange juice
- 5 pounds pork loin
- 2 tablespoons extra virgin olive oil

Directions:

In a bowl, combine the salt, brown sugar, garlic, bay leaves, peppercorns, lemon juice, fennel seeds, pepper flakes, apple juice, and orange juice.

Mix to form a paste rub.

Rub the mixture onto the pork loin and marinate for at least 2 hours in the fridge.

Add in the oil.

When ready to cook, fire the wood pellet grill to 300F.

Use apple wood pellets when cooking.

Close the lid and preheat for 15 minutes.

Place the seasoned pork loin on the grill grate and close the lid.

Cook for 45 minutes.

Make sure to flip the pork halfway through the cooking time.

Pork Collar and Rosemary Marinade

Preparation Time: 15 minutes

Cooking Time: 30 minutes

Servings: 6

Ingredients:

- 1 pork collar, 3-4 pounds
- 3 tablespoons rosemary, fresh
- 3 shallots, minced
- 2 tablespoons garlic, chopped
- ½ cup bourbon
- 2 teaspoons coriander, ground
- 1 bottle of apple ale
- 1 teaspoon ground black pepper
- 2 teaspoons salt3 tablespoons oil

Directions:

Take a zip bag and add pepper, salt, canola oil, apple ale, bourbon, coriander, garlic, shallots, rosemary, and mix well

Cut meat into slabs and add them to the marinade, let it refrigerate overnight

Preheat your smoker to 450 degrees F

Transfer meat to smoker and smoke for 5 minutes, lower temperature to 325 degrees F

Pour marinade all over and cook for 25 minutes more until the internal temperature reaches 160 degrees F Serve and enjoy!

Roasted Ham

Preparation Time: 15 minutes

Cooking Time:2 hours 15 minutes

Servings: 6

Ingredients:

- 8-10 pounds ham, bone-in
- 2 tablespoons mustard, Dijon
- ¼ cup horseradish
- 1 bottle BBQ Apricot Sauce

Directions:

Preheat your smoker to 325 degrees F

Cover a roasting pan with foil and place the ham, transfer to the smoker, and smoke for 1 hour and 30 minutes

Take a small pan and add sauce, mustard and horseradish, place it over medium heat and cook for a few minutes Keep it on the side

After 1 hour 30 minutes of smoking, glaze ham and smoke for 30 minutes more until the internal temperature reaches 135 degrees F

Let it rest for 20 minutes, slice, and enjoy!

Delicious Smoked Loin

Preparation Time: 15 minutes

Cooking Time: 3 hours

Servings: 6

Ingredients:

- ½ quart apple juice
- ½ q uart apple cider vinegar
- ½ cup of sugar
- ¼ cup of salt
- 2 tablespoons fresh ground pepper
- 1 pork loin roast ½ cup Greek seasoning

Directions:

Take a large container and make the brine mix by adding apple juice, vinegar, salt, pepper, sugar, liquid smoke, and stir

Keep stirring until the sugar and salt have dissolved and added the loin

Add more water if needed to submerge the meat

Cover and chill overnight

Preheat your smoker to 250 degrees Fahrenheit with hickory wood

Coat the meat with Greek seasoning and transfer to your smoker

Smoker for 3 hours until the internal temperature of the thickest part registers 160 degrees Fahrenheit Serve and enjoy!

Pulled Pork

Preparation Time: 15 minutes

Cooking Time: 3 hours

Servings: 4

Ingredients:

- 6-9 lb. of whole pork shoulder
- 2 cups of apple cider
- Big game rub

Directions

Set the temperature to 250 degrees F and put it on preheat by keeping the lid closed for 15 minutes

Now take off the excess fat from the butt of the pork and season it with big game rub on all sides

Put the pork butt on the grill grate making sure to keep the fat side up

Smoke it until the internal temperature reaches 160 degrees F. This should take approx. 3 to 5 hours

Remove it from the grill and keep aside

Now take a large baking sheet and keep 4 large pieces of aluminum foil one on top of the other. This should be wide enough to wrap the pork butt entirely

Keep the pork butt in the very center of the foil and bring up the sides a little

Pour apple cider on top of the pork and wrap the foil tightly around it

Keep it back on the grill again having the fat side up and cook till the internal temperature reaches 200 degrees F. This should take 3 to 4 hours approx.

Remove it from the grill and let it rest for 45 minutes inside the foil packet

Take off the foil and pour off the extra liquid

Now keep the pork in a dish and remove the bones and excess fat

Add the separated liq uid back to the pork and season it again with big game rub

Easy Pork Chuck Roast

Preparation Time: 15 minutes

Cooking Time: 4 hours

Servings: 6

Ingredients:

- 1 whole 4-5 pounds chuck roast
- ¼ cup olive oil
- ¼ cup firm packed brown sugar
- 2 tablespoons Cajun seasoning
- 2 tablespoons paprika
- 2 tablespoons cayenne pepper

Directions:

Preheat your smoker to 225 degrees Fahrenheit using oak wood

Rub chuck roast all over with olive oil

Take a small bowl and add brown sugar, paprika, Cajun seasoning, cayenne

Coat the roast well with the spice mix

Transfer the chuck roast to smoker rack and smoke for 4-5 hours

Once the internal temperature reaches 165 degrees Fahrenheit, take the meat out and slice Enjoy!

Sweet Pork BBQ

Preparation Time: 10 minutes

Cooking Time: 60 minutes

Servings: 4

Ingredients:

- 1-pound pork sirloin
- 4 cups pineapple juice
- 3 cloves garlic, minced
- 1 cup carne asada marinade
- 2 tablespoons salt
- 1 teaspoon ground black pepper

Directions:

Place all ingredients in a bowl. Massage the pork sirloin to coat with all ingredients. Place inside the fridge to marinate for at least 2 hours.

When ready to cook, fire the wood pellet grill to 300F. Use desired wood pellets when cooking the ribs. Close the lid and preheat for 15 minutes.

Place the pork sirloin on the grill grate and cook for 45 to 60 minutes. Make sure to flip the pork halfway through the cooking time.

At the same time when you put the pork on the grill grate, place the marinade in a pan and place it inside the smoker. Allow the marinade to cook and reduce.

Baste the pork sirloin with the reduced marinade before the cooking time ends.

Allow resting before slicing.

BBQ Glazed Spareribs

Preparation Time: 10 minutes

Cooking Time: 60 minutes

Servings: 6

Ingredients:

- 3 large spareribs, membrane removed
- 3 tablespoons yellow mustard
- 1 tablespoon Worcestershire sauce
- 1 cup honey
- 1 ½ cup brown sugar
- 13 ounces Traeger Mandarin Glaze
- 1 teaspoon sesame oil
- 1 teaspoon soy sauce 1 teaspoon garlic powder

Directions:

Place the spareribs on a working surface and carefully remove the connective tissue membrane that covers the ribs.

In another bowl, mix the rest of the ingredients until well combined.

Massage the spice mixture onto the spareribs. Allow resting in the fridge for at least 3 hours.

When ready to cook, fire the wood pellet grill to 300F.

Use hickory wood pellets when cooking the ribs.

Close the lid and preheat for 15 minutes.

Place the seasoned ribs on the grill grate and cover the lid.

Cook for 60 minutes.

Once cooked, allow resting before slicing.

Smoked Pork Sausages

Preparation Time: 10 minutes

Cooking Time: 1 hour

Servings: 6

Ingredients:

- 3 pounds ground pork
- ½ tablespoon ground mustard
- 1 tablespoon onion powder
- 1 tablespoon garlic powder
- 1 teaspoon pink curing salt
- 1 teaspoon salt
- 1 teaspoon black pepper
- ¼ cup of ice water
- Hog casings, soaked and rinsed in cold water

Directions:

Mix all ingredients except for the hog casings in a bowl. Using your hands, mix until all ingredients are wellcombined.

Using a sausage stuffer, stuff the hog casings with the pork mixture.

Measure 4 inches of the stuffed hog casing and twist to form into a sausage. Repeat the process until you create sausage links.

When ready to cook, fire the wood pellet grill to 220F. Use apple wood pellets when cooking the ribs. Close the lid and preheat for 15 minutes.

Place the sausage links on the grill grate and cook for 1 hour or until the internal temperature of the sausage reads at 1550F.

Allow resting before slicing.

Braised Pork Chili Verde

Preparation Time: 10 minutes

Cooking Time: 40 minutes

Servings: 6

Ingredients:

- 3 pounds pork shoulder, bone removed and cut into ½ inch cubes
- 1 tablespoon all-purpose flour
- Salt and pepper to taste
- 1-pound tomatillos, husked and washed
- 2 jalapenos, chopped
- 1 medium yellow onion, peeled and cut into chunks
- 4 cloves of garlic
- 4 tablespoons extra virgin olive oil
- 2 cup chicken stock
- 2 cans green chilies
- 1 tablespoon cumin
- 1 tablespoon oregano
- ½ lime, juiced
- ¼ cup cilantro

Directions:

Place the pork shoulder chunks in a bowl and toss with flour. Season with salt and pepper to taste.

Use desired wood pellets when cooking. Place a large cast-iron skillet on the bottom rack of the grill.

Close the lid and preheat for 15 minutes. Place the tomatillos, jalapeno, onion, and garlic on a sheet tray lined with foil and drizzle with 2 tablespoon olive oil. Season with salt and pepper to taste. Place the remaining olive oil in the heated cast iron skillet and cook the pork shoulder. Spread the meat evenly then close.

Before closing the lid, place the vegetables in the tray on the grill rack. Close the lid of the grill. Cook for 20 minutes without opening the lid or stirring the pork. After 20 minutes, remove the vegetables from the grill and transfer to a blender. Pulse until smooth and pour into the pan with the pork. Stir in the chicken stock, green chilies, cumin, oregano, and lime juice. Season with salt and pepper to taste. Close the grill lid and cook for another 20 minutes. Once cooked, stir in the cilantro.

BBQ Pulled Pork Sandwiches

Preparation Time: 10 minutes

Cooking Time: 1 hour 30 minutes

Servings: 6

Ingredients:

- 8-10lbs of bone-in pork butt roast
- 12 Kaiser Rolls
- 1 cup of yellow mustard
- Coleslaw
- 1 bottle of BBQ sauce
- 5 oz of sugar

Directions

Push the temperature to 225 degrees F and set your smoker to preheat

Now take out the pork roast from the packaging and keep it on a cookie sheet

Rub it thoroughly with yellow mustard

Now take a bowl and mix the BBQ sauce along with sugar in it Use this mix to rub the roast thoroughly and give time for the rub to seep inside and melt in the meat Now place this roast in the smoker and allow it to cook for 6 hours When done, remove it from the smoker and then wrap it in tin foil

Push the temperature to 250 degrees F and cook it for a couple of hours. The internal temperature should reach 200 degrees F Let the pork butt rest in the foil for an hour before pulling it out.

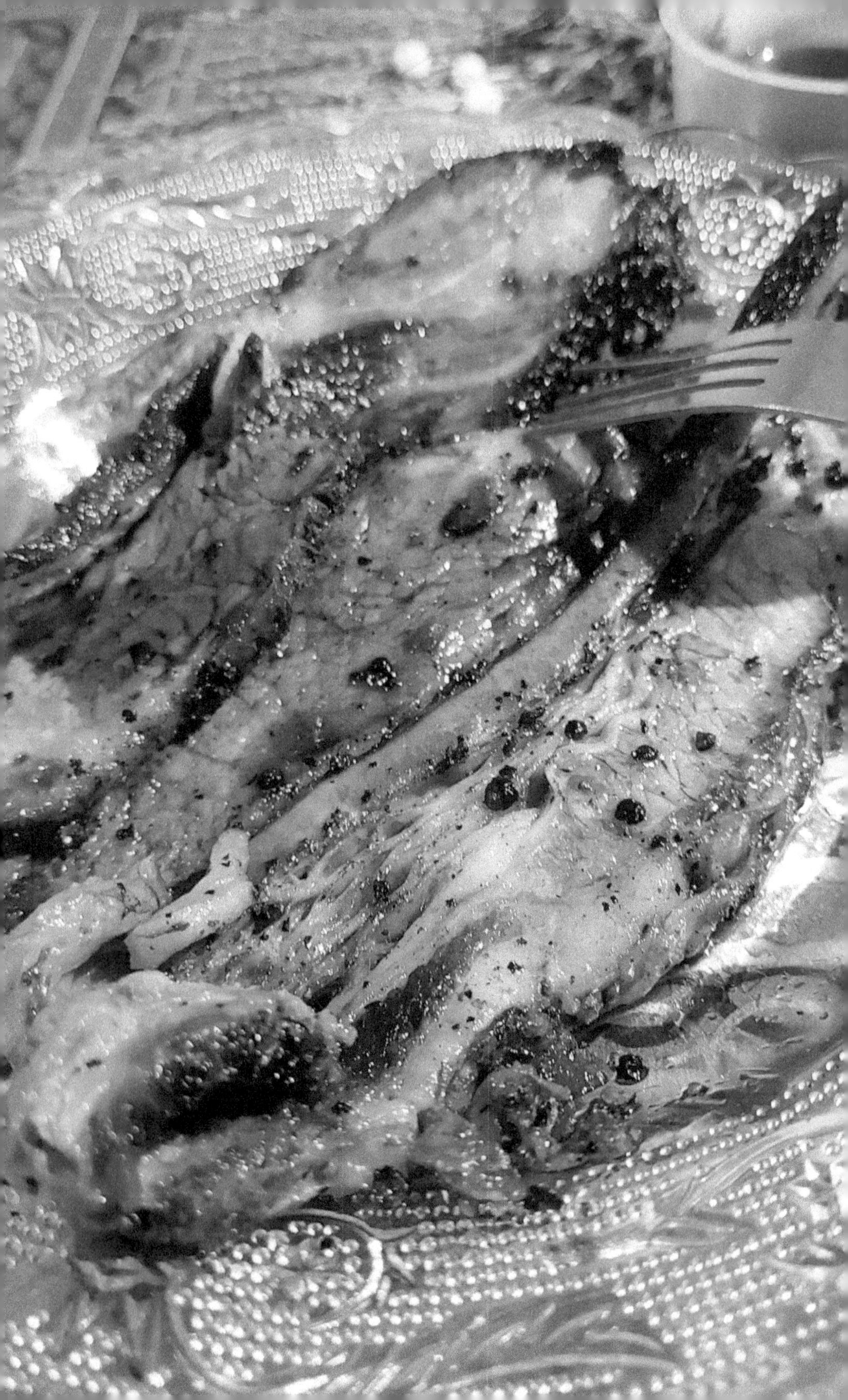

Texas-Style Brisket Rub

Preparation Time: 5 Minutes

Cooking Time: 10 Minutes

Servings: 1

Ingredients:

- 2 tsp Sugar

- 2 Tbsp Kosher salt

- 2 tsp Chili powder

- 2 Tbsp Black pepper

- 2 Tbsp Cayenne pepper

- 2 Tbsp Powdered garlic

- 2 tsp Grounded cumin

- 2 Tbsp Powdered onion

- 1/4 cup paprika, smoked

Directions:

1. Mix all the ingredients in a small bowl until it is well blended.

2. Transfer to an airtight jar or container. Store in a cool place.

Tandoori Chicken Wings

Prep time: 30 minutes | Cook time: 50 minutes | Serves 4

Marinade:
- ¼ cup yogurt
- 1 tablespoon minced cilantro leaves
- 1 whole scallions, minced
- 2 teaspoons ginger, minced
- 1 teaspoon garam masala
- 1 teaspoon ground black pepper
- 1 teaspoon saltWings:
- 1½ pounds (680 g) chicken wings
- Cooking spray

Sauce:
- ¼ cup yogurt
- 2 tablespoons cucumber
- 2 tablespoons mayonnaise
- 2 teaspoons lemon juice
- ½ teaspoon salt
- ½ teaspoon cumin
- ⅛ teaspoon cayenne pepper

1. Place the yogurt, cilantro, scallions, ginger, garam masala, pepper, and salt in a blender and pulse until smooth.

2. Place the chicken wings in a large resealable plastic bag and pour the yogurt mixture over the chicken wings, massaging the bag to coat all the wings. Let marinate for 4 to 8 hours in the refrigerator.

3. Drain the chicken wings of excess marinade, discarding the marinade.

4. When ready to cook, set Traeger temperature to 350°F (177°C) and preheat, lid closed for 10 to 15 minutes. Oil the grill grates with cooking spray.

5. Lay the chicken wings on the grill and cook for 45 to 50 minutes until the skin is crispy, flipping the wings once or twice during cooking.

6. Meanwhile, whisk all the sauce ingredients to combine in a bowl and refrigerate until ready to use.

7. When the wings are done, transfer them to a platter and serve alongside the prepared sauce.

Pan-Roasted Game Birds

Prep time: 10 minutes | Cook time: 1 hour | Serves 6

- 4 pounds (1.8 kg) game birds
- 4 tablespoons melted butter, divided
- Salt and black pepper, to taste
- 2 whole lemon, halved
- 1 bunch fresh thyme
- 1 bunch fresh parsley
- 1 bunch fresh rosemary

1. When ready to cook, set wood pellet grill temperature to high and preheat, lid closed for 15 minutes. Put a large cast iron skillet on the grill while preheating.

2. Rub 2 tablespoons of butter all over the game birds and season the inside and outside with salt and pepper.

3. Stuff the cavity of each bird of half a lemon, a sprig of parsley, thyme, and rosemary. Truss the birds by simply tying the legs together with string.

4. Add the remaining 2 tablespoons of butter to the cast iron skillet on the grill. Place the birds in the hot cast iron skillet and roast for 45 to 60 minutes, or until the internal temperature reaches 165°F (74°C).

5. Rest for 10 minutes before serving.

Glazed Chicken Breasts

Prep time: 20 minutes | Cook time: 30 minutes | Serves 4

- ¼ cup olive oil
- 1 tablespoon Worcestershire sauce
- 1 teaspoon freshly pressed garlic
- Traeger Fin & Feather Rub, as needed
- 4 whole chicken breasts
- ½ cup Traeger 'Que BBQ sauce
- ½ cup Traeger Sweet & Heat BBQ Sauce

1. Whisk together the olive oil, Worcestershire sauce, garlic, and Traeger Fin & Feather rub in a small bowl. Rub the mixture all over the chicken breasts. Combine the both sauces in another bowl and set aside.

2. When ready to cook, set wood pellet grill temperature to 500°F (260°C) and preheat, lid closed for 15 minutes.

3. Arrange the chicken breasts on the grill and cook for 20 to 30 minutes, or until the internal temperature reaches 160°F (71°C) when inserted into the thickest part of the breasts. Glaze the chicken breasts with the sauce mixture during the last 5 minutes of cooking.

4. Remove the chicken breasts from the grill and cool for 5 minutes before serving.

BBQ Half Chickens

Prep time: 15 minutes | Cook time: 1 hour 30 minutes | Serves 2

- 1 (3- to 3½-pounds / 1.4- to 1.6-kg) fresh young chicken
- Traeger Leinenkugel's Summer Shandy Rub
- Traeger Apricot BBQ Sauce, as needed

1. Put the chicken, breast-side down, on a cutting board with the neck pointing away from you. Cut along one side of the backbone, staying as close to the bone as possible, from the neck to the tail. Repeat on the other side of the backbone and then remove it.

2. Open the chicken and slice through the white cartilage at the tip of the breastbone to pop it open. Cut down either side of the breast bone then use your fingers to pull it out. Flip the chicken over so it is skin side up and cut down the center splitting the chicken in half. Tuck the wings back on each chicken half.

3. Season the chicken with Traeger Leinenkugel's Summer Shandy Rub on both sides.

4. When ready to cook, set wood pellet grill temperature to 375°F (191°C) and preheat, lid closed for 15 minutes.

5. Arrange the chicken, skin-side up, on the grill and cook for about 60 to 90 minutes, or until the chicken reaches an internal temperature of 160°F (71°C).

6. Brush all over the chicken skin with Traeger Apricot BBQ Sauce and grill for 10 minutes more.

7. Remove the chicken from the grill and cool for 5 minutes before serving.

Classic Chicken Pot Pie

Prep time: 20 minutes | Cook time: 50 minutes | Serves 4

- 2 tablespoons butter
- 1 stalk celery, diced
- 1 small yellow onion, diced
- 2 tablespoons flour
- 2 cup chicken or turkey stock
- ½ cup milk
- 2 teaspoons dry sherry (optional)
- ½ teaspoon Traeger Pork & Poultry Rub ¼ teaspoon dried thyme leaves
- 1½ cups frozen peas and carrots, thawed
- 4 cups cooked skinless chicken or turkey, diced
- Salt and pepper, to taste
- Cooking spray
- 1 sheet frozen puff pastry
- 1 egg, beaten with 1 tablespoon water

1. When ready to cook, set wood pellet grill temperature to 400°F (204°C) and preheat, lid closed for 15 minutes.

2. In a saucepan over medium heat, melt the butter. Add the celery and onion and sauté for 3 to 5 minutes, or until the onion is translucent. Scatter with the flour and stir to coat.

3. Slowly stream in the chicken stock, whisking out any lumps. Add the milk and bring the mixture to a boil. Allow to simmer for a few minutes until slightly thickened. Whisk in the dry sherry, if desired.

4. Add the Traeger Pork & Poultry Rub, thyme, chicken, and peas and carrots, stirring well. Let simmer for 5 to 10 minutes. Season with salt and pepper to taste.

5. Spritz a cast iron skillet with cooking spray and fill with the pot pie filling.

6. On a lightly floured surface, unroll the puff pastry sheet and let thaw slightly.

7. Cover the top of the cast iron skillet with the puff pastry crimping any overhang. Make several small slits in the center to let the steam escape and lightly brush with the egg wash.

8. Bake for 30 minutes, or until the puff pastry is nicely browned and the filling is bubbling.

9. Let rest for 5 to 10 minutes before serving.

Smoked Turkey with Fig BBQ Sauce

Prep time: 4 hours | Cook time: 2 hours | Serves 2

Brine:
- 1 gallon water
- ½ cup sugar
- ½ cup salt Meat:
- 6 turkey thighs
- ½ cup ras el hanout
- 6 tablespoons extra-virgin olive oil Fig BBQ Sauce:
- 4 fresh figs, stems removed and cut into quarters
- 1 cup Traeger Apricot BBQ Sauce
- 3 tablespoons water, plus more as needed

1. In a large pot, bring the brine ingredients to a boil over high heat, stirring until the sugar and salt are dissolved. Remove from the heat and let cool.

2. Place the turkey thighs in the brine for at least 4 hours or overnight.

3. Remove the turkey thighs from the brine, rinse and pat dry with paper towels.

4. When ready to cook, set wood pellet grill temperature to 250°F (121°C) and preheat, lid closed for 15 minutes. For optimal flavor, use Super Smoke if available.

5. Rub the ras el hanout all over the turkey thighs, then rub each thigh with a tablespoon of olive oil.

6. Place the thighs on the grill and smoke for 2 hours.

7. Meanwhile, make the fig BBQ sauce: In a small saucepan over medium-heat, combine the figs and BBQ sauce. Add the water and cook for 20 minutes, or until the figs are softened, adding more water as needed. Remove what remains of the figs and discard.

8. Remove the thighs from the grill and set aside to rest.

9. Set the temperature to High and preheat, lid closed for 15 minutes.

10. Place the thighs back on the grill and continue to cook, basting occasionally with the fig BBQ sauce, or until the thighs are caramelized and the internal temperature registers 165°F (74°C).
11. Remove the thighs from the grill and baste with the remaining fig BBQ sauce. Serve immediately.

Grilled Lemon Chicken Breasts

Prep time: 5 minutes | Cook time: 15 minutes | Serves 6

Marinade:
- ½ cup olive oil or vegetable oil
- 2 teaspoons honey
- 2 teaspoons kosher salt
- 2 sprig fresh thyme leaves
- 1 lemon, zested and juiced
- 1 clove garlic, coarsely chopped 1 teaspoon freshly ground black pepper Chicken:
- 6 (6-ounce / 170-g) boneless, skinless chicken breasts
- 1 lemon, cut into wedges, for serving

1. In a small mixing bowl, whisk together all the marinade ingredients until well incorporated.
2. Put the chicken breasts in a large resealable plastic bag and pour the marinade over them, massaging the bag to coat the chicken evenly. Marinate for 4 hours in the refrigerator.
3. When ready to cook, set wood pellet grill temperature to 400°F (204°C) and preheat, lid closed for 15 minutes.
4. Remove the chicken breasts from the marinade and drain, discarding the marinade.
5. Place the chicken breasts on the grill and cook until the internal temperature registers 165°F (74°C).
6. If desired, grill the reserved lemon wedges alongside the chicken, cut sides down, about 15 minutes.
7. Transfer the chicken breasts to a platter and serve with the lemon wedges.

Teriyaki Wings

Prep time: 4 hours | Cook time: 1 hour | Serves 6

Chicken:
- 2½ pounds (1.1 kg) large chicken wings
- 1 tablespoon lightly toasted sesame seeds, for serving

Marinade:
- ½ cup soy sauce
- ¼ cup brown sugar
- ¼ cup water
- 2 scallions
- 2 tablespoons rice wine vinegar
- 2 teaspoons sesame oil
- 2 tablespoons smashed fresh ginger
- 1 clove garlic, minced

1. On your cutting board, cut the wings into three pieces through the joints. Discard the wing tips or reserve for chicken stock.
2. Transfer the remaining chicken drumettes and flats to a large resealable plastic bag.
3. In a small saucepan, stir together all the marinade ingredients and bring to a boil. Reduce the heat and allow to simmer for 10 minutes. Let cool to room temperature, then pour the marinade over the chicken wings. Seal the bag and refrigerate for 4 hours or overnight.
4. Remove the wings from the marinade and drain, discarding the marinade.
5. When ready to cook, set wood pellet grill temperature to 350°F (177°C) and preheat, lid closed for 15 minutes.
6. Lay the chicken wings on the grill and cook for 45 to 50 minutes, or until the skin is brown and crisp, flipping the wings once during cooking.
7. Remove the wings from the grill. Serve sprinkled with the sesame seeds.

TEXAS
BARBECUE

- THE -
EST. OLD 1999
TEXAS
PITMASTER
TRAVIS COUNTY

- THE -
EST. OLD 1999
TEXAS
PITMASTER
TRAVIS COUNTY